*DESPERATE CIRCUMSTANCE,
DANGEROUS WOMAN*

*DESPERATE CIRCUMSTANCE,
DANGEROUS WOMAN*

BRENDA MARIE OSBEY

Copyright ©1991 by Brenda Marie Osbey

First American Printing / All rights reserved.

ACKNOWLEDGEMENTS
The first three chapters of this poem originally appeared, in slightly different form, in *2PLUS2: A Collection of International Writing*, published by Mylabris Press International of Switzerland in 1987.
A portion of the first chapter, "Memory," also appeared in *Under 35: The New Generation of American Poets*, a 1989 Anchor/Doubleday publication.
Grateful acknowledgement to those editors.

Published by Story Line Press
Three Oaks Farm
Brownsville, OR
97327-9718

Publication of this book was made possible by the generous support of the Nicholas Roerich Museum, New York.

Library of Congress Cataloging-in-Publication Data

Osbey, Brenda Marie.
        Desperate circumstance, dangerous woman / Brenda Marie Osbey.
                p. cm.
        ISBN 0-934257-57-4: $9.95
        I. Title.
PS3565.S33D47 1991
811'.54—dc20   91-25065
                                                  CIP

CONTENTS

MEMORY	7
REGINA	31
FAUBORG	35
MORNING	39
CEREMONY	45
THE HOUSE IN THE STREET WHERE MEMORY LIVES	53
PROPHECY	61
MANCHAC	65
EVENING	69
REVELATION	75
THE BREAKING OF THE SEASON	85
THE LONG WALK	93
GLOSSARY OF LOUISIANA AND NEW ORLEANS ETHNIC EXPRESSIONS AND PLACE NAMES	98
BIOGRAPHY	105

MEMORY | 7

1.
i sit in the front parlor
the window open from the floor
the hard rain rushing in
stinging like fire-ants
against my feet
the little cloth navy pumps mama had given me
set to one side
out of the wet.

do you know what hunger is?

i sit with the water
moving about my feet
remembering what it feels like to be touched:
my mother's hands parting my oiled hair
down the center
across the front;
my mother's hands bearing down on my back
rolling a little from place to place
as if
there were some secret place she could touch me
to help me cry
and just be done with it;
hands of some hoodoo woman
cradling my face
bathing me in bamba and sweet basil
feeling with her fine wet hands
along my skull
along my spine;
the hands of lovers who thought they knew
something of desire —
good men some of them
with no way of knowing
how their own hands would betray them;

you percy
down on your knees on the hardwood floor
arms wrapped about me
groping with your palms and fingers
along my hips
my thighs:
please woman please
that's what you said
each time you bit my brown flesh
sucking up the little traces of blood
between clenched teeth.
did i cry?
did i cry?
no.
it was you kept saying
you got your hands on me woman
god-have-mercy you got your hands on me
but you stayed
didn't you?

you stayed the night.
you stayed all day the next day.
and when you came back the night after that
you said you couldn't come again
you'd go home to your wife,
do all a man could,
give me anything—
if i'd just take my hands off you.
i remembered your eyes, percy.
i don't know how to beg
that's how you said it
i don't know how to beg
but please
woman please
you got your hands on me and i just can't live like this

you walked out of the house
and across the porch.
you broke off a stem of geranium in the corner.
i saw you press it tight between your fingers.
they smell of iron i said to you then
always smelled of iron to me
like blood percy
like blood

i walked over
to where you crouched above the flowering clay pots.
i put one hand into your near-kinky hair.
percy i said
percy
don't you know what hunger is?

12

2.
the day we buried mama hangs in my mind
like a yellow cotton summer dress
on the clothesline out back.
what i remember?
how her sisters,
the two who outlived her,
argued with me over everything:
the plain wood coffin,
her body,
the clothes i chose to lay her out in,
the ribbon of blue silk
wrapped loosely about her folded hands
which held no meaning for them,
the mexican earrings hanging from her ears,
the mass of grey hair i would not let the mortician dye or
    straighten,
the nails shaped and painted
that moony opal color she wore so often,
and at the wake
the shameless way i touched her
holding
feeling
her hands and face
kissing her eyes and mouth
as though she were a lover
or alive.

that night you lay against me
your face pressed deep
against the pit of my arm.
i rubbed your smooth neck with one hand.
you kissed my breast.
i thought of mama,
the yellow cotton dress
blowing
hanging
on the clothesline

3.
ms. regina stands above me
above my naked body
laid out on the pile of burlap
filled with pungent roots
bruised herbs.
she steps around me in her stocking-feet
sprinkling scented waters
about the burlap
and my skin.
through the long window panes leading up from the floor
i can see
the slates on the rooftops
take on the faint light of a late sun going down.
ms. regina bends and puts both hands
into the earthen vessel beside my head.
she brings out the red cloth
and puts it to my body
begins to rub
slowly
with a back and forth motion
my chest
my breasts
my sides
the soft of my belly
working her way
along the stretch of my body
singing in the same
sing-song voice she uses
for everyday speech.
i go back and forth
between a hard shaking chill
and the calm of yellow cotton dresses.
when ms. regina leaves me

i am thrashing almost to death.
when i wake the next morning
to the smell of thick coffee
and biscuits heavy with butter,
the shades are drawn.
i lie in bed beneath blue cotton sheets and
comforters.
white towels and a wash basin await me
left in plain view
the way a woman ms. regina's age
would remember to place them.
i wash.
i peer into the looking-glass
tilted back against the window ledge.

when i let up the shade to see
there is ms. regina
in the backyard
hanging out the wash.

4.
i sit at my bureau
facing out on the brick and mortar street
and think how your breathing
rattled along your ribs
this morning when i wrapped my legs along your back
coaxing you mercilessly
sideways into me.
i think how it feels to touch
the bony knots along your spine
the way your skin hugs to your frame
the way you look when you open your eyes and say
just take me woman
and be done with it
how you have greyed
the cane you carry
when you walk.

i sit deciding
which letters to write—
the west coast aunts
who bear down on me since mama's death
or the bon fouca cousins
who send pound cake and cane liquor
by parcel post
friends of mama's in point coupée
or the old lover in charleston.
you come in from the side-alley.
marie you call my name.
marie
how long can it take?
just tell me
how much more long?

5.
"the breaking of the season.
if you stand here in the sidelight
you can look over and see it coming from beyond the levee.
any day now
the season will break.
i've told you how your father came to me in the rain.
and you too.
the day you came to me the rain was so heavy
manchac was a sight.
you couldn't tell the swamp from the skies.
i'll bet you didn't remember
to put the water on for my coffee?"

breakfast was ready, i told her
and i was hungry.
she turned from where she stood in the sidelight
to look at me with her light eyes:
"girl
you don't even know what hunger is."
that's what she said.
and that's what i remember.

that same morning she asked me to take a letter.
i thought she meant for me to carry one
to aunt lucille
or a neighbor.
she brought the light blue paper and her best pens.
i remember how my stomach turned weak.
my ears grew hot.
i don't remember
if i thought of papa
gone up to manchac alone
with his gun.
but after that
every letter olender received from her
was in my hand.
i don't know what difference that made
or why i think of it now.

she'd sit across the breakfast table from me
or in the front parlor when it rained.
she sat barefoot, my mother
her bare feet against the hardwood floor.

i don't recall
when i came to accept olender
or the evidence
of my mother's passion in my everyday life.
what i do recall?
those pale blue sheets of paper
the indian mask of her face
that calm dark brown
the light eyes
how she sat
erect
hands loosely folded in her lap
the way she kissed my father every day
putting both hands up to his face
her voice
touch me touch me
i would hear her say to him
standing outside their bedroom door in the evening
all you have to do is touch me.

6.
the wind whips the rainwater across the front parlor floor.
the gate rattles.
large objects are carried on the wind
tossed about frenchmen street.
the sky is bright blue
with only a few tearing clouds
and one streak of coral.
the streets are beginning to flood.
my mother is dead.

"these are the things which are lost to me" she said
"the memory of my own mother.
the middle name she gave me
which my father
your grandfather
took away.
the tears in my father's eyes
when i told him i would marry your father.
olender's trust
when i said to him i would never leave you and your father.
your own innocence.
the use of my hands.
the tamarind tree that bore only bitter fruit i could not eat
or feed to you.
the jar of peaches you threw to the kitchen floor
once when you were six
and angry
because you asked to go to manchac and i said *no*.
did i say i have lost the memory of my own mother?
i've said that.
what more is there?
you look at me. i know what you are thinking—

'the love of men.'
the love of men.
my father was a man.
and your father.
but my middle name? my youth?
the little lean-to up manchac way?
all gone
what is left that remains to me?
only you
and death."

how many years later did she say
"come marie, it's time for my bath"
even though it was the middle of the afternoon
and i helped her into the white porcelain tub
and loosened her braids
catching up the grey mass with a comb,
and when i had finished bathing her
and walked her back to her bed
she sat there naked
and waited until i finished trimming her toenails
and then she pulled at me,
pulled me up close;
she pressed my face against the wide hot space
between her breasts
long and brown and heavy still
because they had only just begun
to sag a little,
and when she released me
i could feel the damp clean smell of her
on my face,
and she kissed me on the lips
and then she died?

7.
what good am i to you?
what good am i?
look at me
at what's become of me
a sack of bones
you think i don't see what's become of my own body?
you think i don't know?
god-have-mercy woman am i a fool and blind too?
he pulled his shirt open then
and showed his hairless chest.
i'm a man he said
i got no breasts
your mother's dead and in the ground
and i'm a man
i got no breast to feed you on
god-have-mercy woman
what use am i to you?
just to lay between your legs all night and struggle?
you got your hands on me good *woman*
but what good comes of it to you?
and think what you doing to me besides

once
when i was twelve or so
i heard ms. regina say these words:
"it's what a woman chooses to remember."
that's all.
that's what i remember.
i think of this while percy stands there
his shirt open
his breathing making that sound.
i look at him.
i think, "i will probably have to put him to bed."
but he reaches for his cane and turns to go.
he stops at my bureau and picks up the letters.
he'll do this errand to get out of this house,
my bedroom,
outside me.

but he knows
and i know
percy will not leave me.

i go behind him.
i stand in the little sidelight.
he stops once he has closed the gate and turns around.
he puts both hands on the gate posts
the cane hanging
sticking out a little.
he is looking at me.
woman he says
woman
i stand and look at him looking at me.
i watch him walk down as far as the street curves
until i can no longer see him.
then i go inside.
i go into the bedroom and take off the shirt i am wearing—
percy's shirt.
i stand before the vanity mirror and look at myself.
i too have no breasts.
no breast to feed on.
do i cry?
no.
and i am a woman.
and this is what *i* remember.

8.
"i have a wife you know.
not any more.
i don't suppose she's my wife anymore.
not after all this.
five children.
four i'm sure of.
but i don't want to know.
don't need to know after all this.
i hardly ever even think about any of them.
it's as if i'd forgotten them
down in my blood.
my blood has forgotten.
it's because of her.

he pauses.
the woman waits for him to go on.
"it's because of her" he says again.
"marie crying eagle.
what kind of name is that for a black woman?"
"faubourg" the woman answers.
"people in the faubourg have all kinds of names.
you know it is the truth.
and what kind of name is good for a black woman?
you know any good names?"
"no" he laughs
"no i guess i don't."
the woman smiles and rubs her hand across her chin.
"everything about her is that way.
she never asked me to leave my wife and children.
never threatened me with them.
she's not like that.
to her it's like they're not alive.
as if i existed all to myself."

"or else" the woman offers
"all to her."

he rolls a cigarette and passes it to the woman.
he rolls another and puts it to his mouth.
percy does not light his cigarette
but talks above it.
"you are an old woman" he says
"but i can say this to you.
she put those skinny arms up around my back
and i went down on my knees.
i can't say what i did or didn't do.
i can't say what i must have promised.
but the first time she put those arms up around me
i was a lost man
and changed.
she's in my blood.
how can a man live
with a full-grown woman
walking in his blood
day and night
day and night?
it's because of her i'm walking on this stick.
i can't walk straight
and carry her in my blood too."

the woman grinds her half-smoked cigarette into the saucer.
she folds a handkerchief
about one hand.
"and you want me to tell you what you must do."
she sucks her teeth a little.
"you are not the first to come to me because of marie crying eagle."
she does not name the names.
"no.
other men have come.
and women too.
the women came to claim their men back.
your wife came some time ago,
back when it all started i suppose.
i told her 'it's marie crying eagle you know.'
she looked out that window there.
'i'm wasting your time then' she said to me.
that's just what she said.
and then she picked up her silver money from the offering plate.
i'm old
and i'm black
but i'm an honest woman.
and that's why i have to tell you
there is nothing i can do for you son.
it's as you say.
she's in your blood.
i can heal
and i can cure.
i can conjure and work roots.
i can even speak in tongues and interpret dreams and signs.
there are not many things i can not do just like you see me.
but i can not take a living woman
from out your blood."

she pushed a tall glass in his direction.
a reddish sediment rests on the bottom.
the liquid is almost clear.
he understands he is to drink from it.
puts the lukewarm glass to his mouth.
"leave some in the bottom" she cautions him.
"good for that ailing side of yours.
see,
i knew you'd come this way.
if not today
maybe tomorrow."
ms. regina takes a long pause and looks away from his face.
"you've heard the tales they tell around frenchmen street" she says,
her words rope thick.
"still you went.
you went to her.
marie crying eagle.
her mother was my best friend once you know."
she sucks her teeth
folds the handkerchief into neat squares.
"with the others it wore away.
not you
because you love her.
you don't say so
and you don't have to.
you knew when you came here you didn't have to tell me.

now smoke your cigarette
and come out to the backyard
and help me bring in this fish i salted down today.
i'll fix you something good to eat.
i can cook too."

REGINA | *31*

if you walk along the rampart
past where it breaks into st. claude
one street back it takes up again.
a little farther on is frenchmen.
and frenchmen takes you nowhere:
not to the river
and not to the bayou.
frenchmen is a place you go to.
you do not walk along its length
going some other place.

but that is another tale
and more than is wise for you to know.
this end of the rampart
people like to tell
how regina went out to the backyard to hang the wash
and when she had strung her mother's bleached sheets
from one end of the yard to the neighboring fence
one hand flew to her head
and she began to dance
stomp barefoot
there in her mother's backyard
for anyone looking to see.

some say she danced till noon.
some say she danced till dark.
but they all say she danced
a young girl
dancing the spirit beneath the clotheslines out back.
no one knows what grief or burden she's paid because of that.

in this part of town
there is a tale for everything.

FAUBOURG 35

the faubourg is a city within the larger city.
and the women walk in pairs and clusters
moving along the slave-bricked streets
wearing print dresses
carrying parcels
on their hips or heads.
within the small city of the faubourg
there is always work to be done:
rooms and yards and laundry to see to
and always some trouble
to be put to rest.
burdens to be shifted
from an arm to a hip
from a hip to the head.
there are children to be scolded and sung to.
there are wares to call out
to sell or buy or search for at market.
and along the narrow banqettes leading there,
a cook
a seamstress
a day's-work-woman to find or be found.
there are chickens to feel and buy
and get their necks wrung.
palm oil to buy and sell
palm wine
hot sweet potato pies.
and there are blues to be sung or heard
above the trees and rooftops
all hours of the day and night.

the dead must be mourned and sung over
and prayers told them to carry to the other side.
the dead must be chanted and marched to their tombs
and the tombs then tended and the dogs kept away.
yatta leaves must be dried and woven into belts and baskets.
rags must be burned in sulphur to ward off mosquitoes
and slave-brick crushed and scrubbed across doorways.
there is love to be made
conju to be worked.

and quiet as it is kept
most anything can be done
in the faubourg.
in such a city
what name is good for a woman?
in such a city
what good is any woman's name?

MORNING

1.
my old man is smoking his morning cigar
sitting out of doors
on the front porch steps.
when he looks up and sees me coming
he stands to meet me at the fence
both hands rubbing the rounded tops of the posts.
i kiss my old man's face across the gate.
he slaps me with his bad hand
and straightens to let me in.
i sit down on the steps where he sat.
he shows me his cigar,
a gesture,
an offer.
i reach for my inside shirt pocket.
"them things'll kill you one day, boy."
i wag my head.
"give you bad breath besides."
i roll my cigarette
and lick the bitter paper end.
i roll the smoking end a while longer,
put it to my lip.
it catches on.
my old man lights me up.
we grin.
he rubs his knee
and catches up a pants leg before sitting again with me.
"how is that skinny woman of yours?

passed here yesterday evening.
guess you know that though.
ain't too much you don't know—
or haven't learned hereabouts lately.
guess i can say what i mean.
i'm an old man, boy.
old, old man."
i flick the butt into a green hedge.
"marie don't change much, old man" i tell him.
"nòn" he says.
"nòn.
i wouldn't think she did.
wouldn't think she did.
but then you know what you doing.
(*a grunt*)
only one knows."
my old man holds out his cigar.
shows it to me
like some new thing he is just now seeing.

"me? i don't claim wisdom or knowledge" he offers.
"just live a long time is all."

2.
it is morning.
early.
we sit and smoke and watch the city come alive—
windows going up
the smell of hot frenchbread
of grits and eggs and coffee
fresh soap and mavis talcum.
next door ms. lonnie is cursing
soon as the radio comes on.
and somewhere down the street
around a corner
somebody,
a child,
is teasing a dog.
screen doors will start to open and slam shut.
gaggles of small children
in plaid or navy or khaki uniforms
will start their daily processions
to buses and schools and forbidden sweet shops.
you wouldn't think it.
but there are so many men inside this city.
the old ones sit on porch steps
stand on corners
morning
evening
all hours of the day.
they talk or smoke or point with chins or fingers
and never seem to be waiting on anything.
the younger men
in dark pants or khakis
drive trucks, a few cars
the steamy red and cream-colored buses

that only ever break down in the awful heat of summer.
the younger men stop at their mother's houses
for coffee and hard frenchbread.
they sit or stand and stir the syrupy liquid about.
they talk about the weather
something a friend, some other man,
said or did or didn't do.
sometimes they hand their mothers money—
soft, damp bills rolled into folds a little while ago.
and when they have no money to hand over
they laugh hardier
ask more questions
sit or stand
a little longer.
and all the while
somewhere out of doors
neighbor-women are pouring out of houses
in check or flower-print dresses.
you can hear their off-beat chorus of good-mornings—
the blue and brown and yellow voices.
all day they will come and go
walking their own or someone else's children to school,
themselves or some elder to a bank or a doctor,
on their way to work or to market
to mass or ms. regina's.

i am leaning near the front porch steps with my old man.
my mother is somewhere inside
singing.

CEREMONY | *45*

1.
"i didn't come here about any mess with percy.
and i don't much care what was said or done or any of that.
i have more respect for you than that.
i think you know that.
you were my mother's friend, ms. regina.
and i'm in no position to ask you *any*thing."

she does not look away, across the room.
what kind of woman
and what name?
her hands fold together across the small table.
her hands bathe lives in roots and promises.
her hands call to the dead and speak their tongue
keep equal time with good and evil
weighing out her days:
ailment of the spirit
ailment of the body—
basil
sweet bamba—
what bark or root or blessèd word of promise?

"i won't stay if you have work.
i won't keep you from your seekers.
but maybe some coffee.
some of your coffee
would be nice.

bamba
sweet basil
the sounds of leaves shifting just beyond a curtain
that impossible shade of blue sky
and morning rising all around and moving.

what ceremony
and what name is good?

2.
i am an old woman and not ready to die.
i am an old woman
and love and death and revenge and lies
all come to sit at my table.
sometimes it takes a little something—
a little parsley water
a little palm wine—
just to set my blood moving in my body.
but old as i am
and just like you see me,
they come in droves.
they come with their silver money
and their hot plates of food.
palm wine or bourbon or tobacco for offering.
they come
and then they go.

and i have been hearing my name in this street since i was a girl."
she pours the coffee
stirring in cream and lump brown sugar
without touching bottom
or looking away.

"my daddy was a building man.
helped build that house you live in.
built this house for mama and his mama.
and every child mama carried in this house died before term.
i am my daddy's only living seed."
she pauses here
and looks away.
"never called me by my name inside this house.
called me child-of-mine till the day he died.
never called my name.
my whole life."

49

and in a higher tone:
"i was the stone in my daddy's crown.
and my mama never spoke a hard word to me.
never.
anybody ask about my people
that's what i tell.
and that's what is true.
what i remember.
and it never will be any different.
dead and gone and *still* the same.

same with your people.
same with you.
it's what you hold to in your middle makes your memory.
and only you can know what's in your memory, baby.
and if you got a danger living in you
then you go to take it by the hand
and walk with it.
live with it.
you got to *live* with your danger, daughter."

3.
the silence left by this woman's voice
is soft and damp.
the silence this woman makes leaves almost nothing
untouched.
inside.
outside.
the walls of these houses set close together
breathe and sweat
like a gang of men working long- and short-time down on the docks.

it is almost summer.
if you walk along this inside street
you can feel the breathing of these houses set so close together
only a little ways back from the river.
some houses breathe deeper
harder
than the rest.
and night has fallen
a heavy sweating caul of night
fallen
fallen
like a shroud.

THE HOUSE
IN THE STREET
WHERE MEMORY LIVES | 53

1.
i am sitting on a chair in the front parlor
the window open
from the floor.
i am waiting for a vision.
but no vision will come.
this is the place my mother sat
walked
bare feet touching
the hardwood floor.
her eyes hold rain
and the memory of rain.
her eyes hold rain when there is no rain.
and the heavy tenderness underneath.
the heavy scent she pressed on me.
and no one answers
and the walls turn in
and look on me.

*where have you been
in all this weather?*

2.
far in the night
far off in the blue swamp
an old man is prancing
knees high
first one
then the other.
he moves about a bit of raised earth.
he wears a thin blue shirt
hand-worked in gold.
he wears leggings and short rubber boots.
he holds a piece of bark in one hand
a small pouch in the other

everything in its place, she said to him

his knees go up then down.
he makes the half-circle
spins
turns away.
the song he is singing
contains no words i might know.
and i am standing on a raft
that is not moving.
and the raft is on the water
and the water does not move.

everything in its place she said

i am not moving.
the old man croons, steps, motions around me.
this is not the vision
i had hoped for.

3.
i sit at the front parlor window.
i touch memory with the tips of my fingers
the back of my tongue—
it falls apart.
the old woman.
the man who is old now and alone up a manchac.
alone in all that swamp—
it falls apart.
memory
the years and all their days
rolling a little from place to place
the visions that dry before they can be grasped
visions that dance in the hard sunlight
stretched long across the floor.

bamba
sweet basil
the stocking-feet of my mother's friend
the good hands of a man
death and betrayal
the turning away
small senseless words like *please*—
what good is any of this to me now?
to anyone?
it falls apart.
it falls.

here is my chest all bone and fleshless skin
with almost no breast to cling to
my hips below
my belly
hands of a woman
hands of a man
it is falling.
it is falling now.
far far into the night
it falls
bamba sweet basil
the thrashing of bones
the witch of sleep
the caul come down.
and there is the city, the street.
here, the house my mother built.
the house my mother built around us
asks the same questions my mother asked.

i do not answer.
this is my house.

4.
the house in the street where memory lives
sits back from the curb.
a small frontyard
clusters of camellias
low flowering hedges spread here and there
two paths leading back to side-alleys:
one paved over
the other tamped earth where almost nothing grows.
the quarter-gallery sets it off from the other houses in this street.
the only such gallery here,
screened all about.
a door to latch midway
slide-lock below.
this house was built and re-built
by a family of men
to suit the needs of a woman
with little to hide.
a woman who is dead and buried now
in a wall-vault with her husband.
a house of wood and plaster
and heavy doors opening from the floors.
a house where some rooms sit vacant, still
altogether empty:
fireplace and mantle
and the windows opening from the floors.
as in ordinary rooms

there are voices
and shadows
and the grey balls of dust that collect in corners.
but tonight
these sounds are covered.
a man.
a woman.
whatever other sounds this house might make.
covered
drowned out by his voice calling and reaching
her voice returning
and the smell of their sweat
seeping into the listening walls
traveling out of the house
into the lighted streets
where memory waits.

in one corner
a man's cane is leaning.
and morning comes.
and then it goes.

5.

woman woman
you keep telling me.
but i just know what i know.
like the man in the song says:
"i only know
what i know, lord."
i walk up behind you standing there in the back door.
i see the hairs standing out fine on your arms and legs.
i hear my own breathing
like when i climb into you in the night.
i feel the blood go to my head.
i walk up on you standing there in the kitchen door.
you turn around
could be you're right.
not as if you ever *did* me any harm.
but then you never had to.
what you put on me
you put on me day-one.
i sit down at the table, push back my sleeves.
and when you turn around
there's not a speck of kindness in your face for me.

PROPHECY | *61*

it comes to this then:
sacrament
ritual
the casting of nets on muddied waters
the long walk back
bended knees
the taking and giving of blessings.
i was a young woman
and now i am old.
i see the things the young can not see.
i turn my eyes in on my heart.
don't let me put my hands to dirt, i pray
don't let me put my hands to dirt
i am old
too old maybe even for this vision.
and surely too old
to deal in contradiction—
good and evil
body and spirit
earth, air, water, seed—
everything in its own place
everything.

i dance these steps the young can not learn.
and if i ever learned to dance the spirit in my youth i do not
    remember.
i sit and see what i do not see.
i bend my knees and press my lips to earth and grass and pray:
don't let me put my hands to dirt
and when i stand and look out from my chapelroom window
there are misbelieve and fig
parsley and ripe tomato
and the yellow roses my daddy planted for his offering.
i go into the frontroom
and stand and look out at nothing in particular.
outside
the street is empty.
i stand and watch the lamppost lights.
they flicker and almost flutter in their own half-light.
i open wide my frontdoor
and stand inside the wavy pool of light.

it's like the old folk say i say.
blood will tell
truth will out

MANCHAC | 65

twenty-eight miles of alligator and murky water.
what passes for a road—
a build-up of ancient sod hard as stone
a scant two feet above,
natural or man-made
no one bothers to recall.
manchac pass the maps read for a year or two—
after the department of streets or highways
the levee board or else some governor's office
thought to throw on a truckload of shell and name it that.
except the name never took.
nobody between here and the state line ever called it that.
nobody nearabout
ever bothered to call it anything at all.
a cut-off.
one of several possible cut-offs on the way to mississippi.
and who-the-hell leaves here
headed for mississippi?
twenty-eight miles of swamp and pitch-darkness.
no sign.
no light.
perhaps one other car
if you are lucky
and start out before suppertime.
but going full speed
heading back to the city
in the opposite direction.

a dirt and shell road raised just above the water.
twenty-eight miles going.
twenty-eight miles coming back.
swamp manchac
is a damp
and lonely
and dangerous
crossing.

EVENING | 69

1.
"i can not tell you what we talk of when we talk."
she looks into his eyes and does not look away.
"and you know you have no right to ask.
besides,
it would not help you get her back into the city
what little i do know.
it would not straighten your right side
or take the hunger from out your middle."
she pauses here
but does not look away.
"i can tell you this,
if it's any consolation to you—
i can tell you you will die years before marie crying eagle ever does.
and you won't be dead any time too soon.
you'll live.
and she'll live longer.
and i wonder
if that knowledge helps you any,
son."

2.
he stands and empties his trouser pockets onto the table.
he separates the paper money from the silver
and puts the paper back into his pockets.
the silver he takes up without counting.
he takes the old woman's left hand
crosses her palm
with two rows of silver coins.
he steps over to the burlap matting
and strips away his clothes.
the old woman,
eyes averted,
holds up a pale blue cotton sheet.

for the first time perhaps,
as he bends to take off shoes and socks,
he sees she is a small woman
and that she seems—
at least in this light—
older than he thought.

she winds the sheet about him without looking.
he gathers up his skirts
and kneels onto the burlap at her feet.
her own feet are covered in stockings
but the anklets and painted nails show through.
when it is done—
the questions and their proper or improper responses,
his tongue stumbling over the unfamiliar words,
her dance about his outstretched form,
the purification—
when it is done
and he is walking home,
this is what he will recall of this afternoon:

that it was a wednesday evening,
that the room smelled of bitter herbs,
and the copper bracelets
and painted toenails
of ms. regina's small feet.

1.
"well.
i guess you come a long ways.
from the city?
treacherous drive, that.
yes ma'am."
he pushes the blue-grey cap back from his forehead.
he looks her over
but his eyes stay firm.
"yes *ma'am*.
all the way out from the city
and nobody home.
i wish i could help you, miss.
but to tell the truth,
i do know how you feel.
story of my life.
in fact,
i was kinda hoping you'd be the lady of the house.
yeah.
and this's been my route since '40, '41."
he sits down on the steps
and makes himself comfortable.
"cigarette?"
she shakes her head.
"no.
no, thank you."
leans against the door jamb
as if she too
intends to wait.
the postman gathers his knees up higher,
pulls a pall mall from its pack with his teeth,
the mail pouch nestled
one step below,
leather strap
slung loose about one knee.
"yes ma'am," he says.

"i sure was hoping you'd be the lady of the house.
these people kin to you?"
for the first time
she looks directly into his face.
"no" she says softly.
"no. not really."

one, two brief moments
she considers.
"people" she says after a while.
"you said *people*.
who else lives here?
i mean,
is there more than one person?"
"far as i know
could be hundreds of 'em.
far as i *know*.
i been the regular man on this route since '41
and i ain't see a soul.
that's right.
not a soul.
so i don't suppose you'd be the one
always picks up the mail then?"
"no" she says again.
"no.
my mother.
my parents.
they're dead.
but they knew him.
but that was all a long time ago
and maybe it's not even the same person.
this might be the wrong house.
i thought i could find it
without much trouble
but this might be the wrong house."

he slips an envelope from his bag.
the envelope is not quite blue.
more grey than blue.
she looks down quickly
and looks away.
he's seen her, though.
in that one brief moment
he's seen her face change.
he's seen her look
and look away.
the stem of ash on his cigarette
lingers a long moment,
lengthens,
falling all at once
on the wooden step between his two feet.
he holds the envelope up and reads aloud,
"mr. r. t. olender
gulf lane road.
that your man?" he smiles.
she looks straight ahead
saying nothing.
"oh." his smile gone now.
no offense, ma'am.
i just meant
was he the one you looking for?
he the one your people said they knew?"
"my people" she echoes.
"yes. yes he is.
that's right.
olender."

she would have closed her eyes
but they would only flutter open again
having memorized
the store of fine blue paper
the pens her mother's father had given her
the silver nibs
the deep blue ink
indigo
against the pale blue sheets:
dear olender...
she rubs her hands
up and down both arms.
her red dress is long-sleeved
but she can feel the hair
sense it standing out
against the cloth of her dress.
it is not cold.
and here in the swamp country
it is already spring.

she looks again at the postman.
he smokes his pall mall.
he seems contented.
he *is* contented.
"my name's walker, miss" he smiles
somewhere in her direction.

"marie" she says.
"marie crying eagle."
"nice name.
nice name for a nice lady."
"you think so, mister walker?"
"oh, just plain walker, miss.
walker st. john.
but everybody calls me walker."
he stretches his legs out,
laughs,
at home with himself
on the unclaimed porch
of mr. r. t. olender.
"that's another thing i was hoping today,
miss marie.
hoping to see you smile."
he pulls his cap down again
flexes his ankles
the white cotton socks showing
and just above
the matte-black of his narrow legs
crossed at the ankles.
walker the postman
is content.

looking again out into the road
marie smooths her skirt behind
and sits one step higher.
"some neighbors drove me in from the city" she offers.
"it'll be a few hours still
before they pass back."

2.
"you say you've been delivering mail around here a long time
but you've never met olender?
you wouldn't have any idea where he would be?
he must be way too old
to go wandering too far or too long.
what about the other people around here.
don't they know him?"
she rises from the step and looks about.
"maybe somebody can tell me when he'll be back."
he laughs
yanks his legs up high again.
"miss marie.
i don't mean to laugh
but you really, *really* city-folk.
let walker tell you, miss marie,
the last thing these maroon people do
is tell some stranger,
even a nice stranger from the city like you,
where anybody—
especially this mr. r. t. olender—
has gone to
and when or if he's coming back."

"i'm not exactly a stranger" she says.
"i told you
my people used to know him."
"and they never told you not to come out here
hoping to find him
here
at this house?" he is smiling.
she is a young woman.
younger than she knows.
especially today.

she sits again on the upper step
and stares into the face of the postman
enjoying his own chuckle.
"what did you call this place?"
"not the place
the people.
these people all along this road
far as you can see
and farther on,
every last one of them is maroon.
at least they come from maroons.
or their people did."

when he turns to look at her with his smile
he sees she does not understand.
"you mean you don't know about the maroons?
you think i'd be out here in the sticks
these sticks—
if my old man wasn't *ma-ròn,* as we say?
not a thing in these swamps for a young man these days.
but you really don't know,
do you?
she looks directly into his smooth
matte-black face.
she looks directly into his chestnut-colored eyes.
"i have time" marie crying eagle says softly.
"nothing but time.
tell me what you know.
tell me walker.
please."

THE BREAKING OF THE SEASON

marie sits tall and very quiet
in the back seat of verde barthelme's car
by sheet force of will
or memory
whatever it is.
verde's woman léanna
has given up trying to engage and distract her.
as they near the faubourg
marie's voice sounds in verde's direction.
"i'd like to get down at the market, mr. v,
get a chicken or something from steve's."
but before he can respond
léanna begins her protest.
the rain is going to break any minute.
it's best to go straight on.
who can say how hard this one will be?
"i'll get down at the market" she says
as if she had not heard.
there is the merest wrinkle of thunder.
the lightning is like thin strips of aluminum
yanked in and quickly out of the greying sky.
when the car pulls up to the curb and stops
marie steps down.
"thank you" she says
and turns away.
two steps gone,
she turns back.
leans into the wind on verde's side
léannna's face looming disapproval.
"don't wait for me.
please.
you-all go in out this weather.

i can walk home from here.
i need a chicken,
one or two things for percy and me."

barthelme tips his hat slightly
drives on,
léanna still talking.
inside the market
marie carries a yellow-painted pannièr.
onion, a string of garlic, sweet bell pepper.
tomatoes from ms. lonnie's yard
are still ripening in the kitchen window.
fresh parsley, basil, hot peppers, string beans.
a small brown sack of long-grain rice.
she pays the old woman standing at the entryway
of the st. claude market.

"you the last one out here in this weather buying supper, marie.
you better get on in before it starts.
me, i'm closing for the day."
"what about steve?" she wants to know.
"the coop closed down for the day yet?
i need a chicken or something for percy's supper."
"that old cheapskate round there, girl,
counting his pennies.
but *you* best get out this weather.

she turns the corner onto the rampart.
steve's coop is loaded down with hens of different colors.
they too seem to marie
to be waiting on the weather.
as usual steve says nothing
grunts in her direction
pointing to those birds nearer the front.
marie ignores him
veers to the st. claude street side of the coop
and reaches her hand in
to feel among the plumper breasted birds sitting and standing there.
the old man grunts again
reaches a tobacco-brown hand in to grasp the one she's chosen.
she stands aside
looking on as he wrings the bird's neck
beheads it
plunges it into one of several steaming buckets
and hands it over to his nephew to pluck and gut and clean.

the smell of warm blood and feathers comes up sharp
then drifts.
the first huge drops of rain
are spattering against the sheet metal roof
of steve's corner chicken coop.
the old man hands her the bird
and change back from her silver dollar
counting twice—
once for his benefit
and again for hers
silent
except for the grunt that says everything
and nothing
according to his own need
or the time of day.

the sky is dark purple where the clouds appear to meet
rushing together faster than marie can walk.
the rain comes in great drops
against her head
the panniér loaded down with supper
the street.
along the rampart
windows, doors, their sidelights and jalousies
are closed
battened down against the rain that will break the season
bringing spring into the city like a shout.

the flames of the street lamps leap inside their globes
and through the closed lid of the panniér
comes the smell of the still-warm chicken
fresh from the killing
that she carries on one arm.
inside the house where memory lives and breathes
a man stands in the middle of the frontroom floor.
he walks to the window facing the street,
the window that is always open from the floor.
he leans his cane against the wall nearby.
he puts the heels of both hands against the window's lower
    ledge
pulls once
sharply down
in one slow movement
he steps
and turns away from the huge paned glass
streaked now with the hard slashes of rain.
he moves to where the chair rests

and pulls it to the opposite side.
his cane against the frontroom wall,
the window pulled to but unlocked,
he positions himself to see her coming
looking out past the streaked panes
into the street.
he is patient.
he is no longer young.
he sits.
he watches.
waits.
down at her end of the rampart
an old woman stands with her door wide open,
her stocking-feet shoved into carpet slippers
faded to an irridescent no-color
something like stale green or purple.
her black fingers bruise the bitter herbs she carries in both pockets—
the stuff of her trade
the work that has kept debt
and doctors and fools from her door all these years
only to surround her
with the life's-trouble of every man and woman she has known
since the youth spent as her father's jewel
in the house where he never spoke her name—
death,
fear, soul-sickness,
the lesser evils—

she turns her back on the street,
the rain blowing hard
first one way
and another.
she latches the door.
night is early tonight.
and the season
is breaking.

she passes through the chapelroom her father made
while she was still a virgin
and a girl.
she kneels briefly before the altar-shrine
pressing head and hands to the white cloth
between her and the floor and the ground below.
rising on her knees
she crosses shallow breasts with both arms
and stands to leave
snuffing out the day's candles as she goes
and emptying her pockets
onto the floor.
night comes early tonight, she reminds herself
taking bones older than she remembers
on to bed for the night.
and once settled between the white sheets and comforters
of her parents' bed,
emptied of the day's contradictions,
she does not stir
but settles,
an old woman,
and small,
settled
for the night.

the winds and rains have come into the city
swelling the levees to overflowing in parts
all but emptying the streets of the faubourg
where the land is low
and a few more bricks lodge loose from mud or mortar,
where the houses absorb their fair share
as the streets slope to meet the banqettes
and the water pools.
next will come the brief cold snap—
a week, ten days—
but not yet.
for now there is the rain
crashing along the slave-bricked streets,
sputtering against
the slated rooftops
of the faubourg.

and out in the weather
marie rounds the corner onto the street where she lives
where she has lived
twenty-seven-and-a-half years a daughter.
in her eyes is a vision:
an old man
stepping
and the song he sings
without a single word she might know.
and the raft is on the water.
and the water does not move.
rain.
and the memory of rain.
she looks up at the frontroom window—
a gesture
a motion—
and when she reaches the step
this end of the long walk back,
there is percy at the door
reaching her in from the outside with one arm
the other rooted to his cane,
and her wet through to the bone.
his eyes find hers
set deep in their sockets
chestnut brown
the color ma-ròn
somewhere between the camelback house here on frenchmen
and an eternity of hunger
danger
nothing but vision
somewhere out manchac way.

Glossary of Louisiana and New Orleans Ethnic Expressions and Place Names

anklet: ankle bracelet of bronze, gold or silver, traditionally worn on the left foot by New Orleans hoodoo women

altar-shrine: a large altar-like structure holding and containing a variety of sacred objects and images, relics, statuary, candles, etc.; usually the focal piece of a Hoodoo chapel or chapel-room, traditionally constructed to face eastward

banqette: paved or boarded sidewalk

bayou: any of the marshy inlets or outlets of lakes and other bodies of water throughout Louisiana; the bayou referred to here is Bayou St. John, located in downtown New Orleans and, for Black New Orleanians, a traditional meeting place for rituals and festivals

Bon Fouca: formerly a small farming area outside the city-limits of New Orleans, now a sub-division of Slidell, Louisiana

the breaking of the season: the annual and often torrential rains immediately preceding spring and autumn, traditionally recognized as the beginning of the new season and often accompanied by high winds and street flooding; spirtually the rains, and the seasons they announce, symbolize birth, death, transformation, etc.

can liquor: a heavy, rum-like alcoholic beverage distilled from sugar cane, manufactured and drunk by slaves throughout Louisiana and much of the Caribbean and Latin America; it was also frequently used as offering or libation

chapel-room: that room, usually in the home of Hoodoos and Spiritualists, devoted to religious and spiritual practice and consultation

the City: New Orleans; a common usage among those born and raised in New Orleans and for whom rural Louisiana often is unknown or mistrusted as a kind of backwater wilderness

conju: a reference to the practice of conjuring or other spiritual trade and practice associated with Hoodoo

to cross the palms (of someone): it is common practice for petitioners seeking the services of a Hoodoo woman with hard cash; to do so is not considered payment, but largely a symbolic gesture demonstrating faith

to cross (one's) arms: a way of blessing oneself before, after and during Hoodoo ritual or when passing a sacred place, similar to the Catholic tradition of making the sign of the cross

(from or since) day-one: folk expression meaning early, since the beginning

day's-work-woman: a maid, laundry-woman or other woman servant hired and paid a small wage for a single day or half-day; during 18th and 19th centuries, poorer free Black women hired themselves out to wealthier women, Black and white, in this manner and could frequently be found at any of the open marketplaces around New Orleans; this practice continued well into the early 20th century in some areas of the city

faubourg: any of the early, named suburbs and districts in New Orleans, such as the Faubourg Marigny, the setting of this poem, or the nearby Faubourg Tremè

(to have or put one's) hands on (someone or something) to use conjure or Hoodoo to influence the behavior of another or the outcome of a situation; the expression usually carries negative, or even evil, connotations

Hoodoo: in New Orleans and much of southeast Louisiana, a religious and spiritual belief system governing and encompassing all life and life principles including, but not limited to rituals, mysteries, healing, protection from evil, conjuring, interpretations of dreams and signs as well as proper care of the dead and ritual veneration of ancestors; the fundamental practice and principles of Hoodoo are West African and Caribbean in origin; unlike the Caribbean practice of Voodoo or Obeah, there is in New Orleans no longer any group ritual or ceremony; conju women and others who function as priestesses or "mothers" are referred to as "Hoodoos"; the term is also used, loosely, as a verb, e.g. to hoodoo or be hoodooed by someone (a folk usage, often negative in connotation)

jalousies: permanent wooden shades made of narrow horizontal slats that slope and overlap, used to keep out sun and heat while admitting light and air; in New Orleans, jalousies or other shutters frequently cover all entries, including doors, *sidelights* and windows

lean-to: a small, usually one-room, house with sloping roof; so called because part of the roof is typically attached to a larger building, tree or other support; a common structure in rural Louisiana and older areas of New Orleans

levee: in New Orleans, one of the paved, boarded or grassy embankments along the network of canals designed to prevent flooding should the Mississippi River rise; levees were also frequently the sites of ritual and recreational gatherings

Manchac: a large and once desolated swamp tract, situated west of Lake Pontchartrain and said, by some reports, to have functioned in the past as a haven for runaway slaves and other fugitives; also known both as Manchac Swamp and Swamp Manchac

Manchac Pass: a once unpaved dirt and shell road originating west of Lake Pontchartrain and eventually leading north to the Louisiana/Mississippi state line, eventually paved over and appearing on maps as Highway 51, and now a seldom used scenic route

ma-ròn: Creole for *maroon* ; also, the dark chestnut or reddish-brown skin color typical of maroons

maroon: an escaped slave or a community of escaped slaves secluded in the wilderness, forest or swamp lands; in Louisiana, maroons and their descendants were often believed to possess special knowledge or power of a spiritual nature or to bear special access to African ancestors and therefore regarded with awe and feared by some

misbelieve: New Orleans apellation for the japanese plum tree common throughout the area; a mild table wine, sometimes used as a curative, is made from the bright orange fruit

pannièr: any large basket made of wood, straw or cane and equipped with handles and a lid, used for transporting groceries and other small market goods

parsley water: a highly concentrated beverage made by steeping crushed leaves of the herb parsley; alternately used as a palliative and to cleanse and invigorate the body

quarter-gallery: Louisiana designation for the semi-circular porch attached to one side and the front or back of a large house; accessible from the house and surrounding yard or garden

seekers: those who seek the aid, assitance or counsel of conju women, Hoodoos and Spiritualists

side-alley: the paved or unpaved passageway on one or both sides of a house and separating it, with or without a wall, fence or hedge, from neighboring houses and yards and providing access to a side or rear entrance

sidelight: one of the two narrow doors on either side of the main door to a house; a common architectural feature in New Orleans, sidelights are generally left open during warm weather months for added ventilation and easy access to the outdoors and thus typically used to observe the activities of neighbors and passers-by

slave-bricked: descriptive of any road, street, building or other structure constructed all or in part of the common red brick found throughout New Orleans and originally manufactured by slaves employed by the St. Joe Brick Factory; because these bricks were the handiwork of slave ancestors, they are believed to possess spiritual powers and most frequently used to bless and purify the homes of the faithful by rubbing across doorways; slave-brick is also used for drawing vèvè's (religious symbols) on stone, wood, paper, etc.

stomp barefoot: without shoes or hose of any kind; completely barefoot

sulphur burning: in those areas of New Orleans near canals, lagoons and other waterways, it was common practice well into the 1960's to burn rags covered with powdered sulphur to ward off mosquitoes and swarming insects at night

tamarind: a tropical tree bearing small date or fig-like fruit

wall-vault: a large or small family tomb built into the stone, brick and plaster walls of the above-ground cemeteries of New Orleans

yellow cotton: a light weight, unbleached cotton or muslin used to make napkins, dishcloths, hand towels, girls' and women's summer nightgowns and shifts or other simple house-dresses

ABOUT THE AUTHOR

Brenda Marie Osbey is a native of New Orleans. She received the B.A. from Dillard University, the M.A. from the University of Kentucky and attended the Universitè Paul Valèry at Montpèllièr, France. Her poems have appeared in numerous journals, anthologies and collections including *Callaloo, Obsidian, Essence Magazine, Southern Exposure, Southern Review, Woman Poet: the South, Early Ripening: American Women's Poetry Now, The Made Thing: an Anthology of Contemporary Southern Poetry, 2PLUS2: A Collection of International Writing, The Greenfield Review, TENDRIL, Epock, American Voice* and *The American Poetry Review*. She was awarded the Academy of American Poets Loring-Williams Award, a 1984 AWP (Associated Writing Programs) Poetry Award, and has been a fellow of the MacDowell Colony, the Fine Arts Work Center in Provincetown, the Kentucky Foundation for Women, the Millay Colony and the Bunting Institute of Radcliffe College, Harvard University. She is the recipient also of a 1990 National Endowment for the Arts Creative Writing Fellowship. She has taught French and English at Dillard University in New Orleans and African American and Third World literatures at the University of California at Los Angeles.